Greater Than a Tourist - Koblenz
Rhineland - Palatinate
Germany

50 Travel Tips from a Local

Hiral Doshi

Order Information: To order this title please email lbrenenc@gmail.com or visit GreaterThanATourist.com. A bulk discount can be provided.

Lock Haven, PA

All rights reserved.

ISBN: 9781521884706

>TOURIST

Hiral Doshi

BOOK DESCRIPTION

Are you excited about planning your next trip? Do you want to try something new while traveling? Would you like some guidance from a local? If you answered yes to any of these questions, then this book is just for you.

Greater Than a Tourist by Hiral Doshi offers the inside scope on Koblenz. Most travel books tell you how to travel like a tourist. Although there's nothing wrong with that, as a part of the Greater than a Tourist series, this book will give you travel tips from someone who lives at your next travel destination.

In these pages you'll discover local advice that will help you throughout your stay. This book will not tell you exact addresses or store hours but instead will give you an excitement and knowledge from a local that you may not find in other smaller print travel books. Travel like a local. Slow down, stay in one place, and get to know the people and the culture of a place.

By the time you finish this book, you will be eager and prepared to travel to your next destination.

Hiral Doshi

TABLE OF CONTENTS

20. Check out some old train models at Deutsche Bahn Musuem

21. Sneak Peak at Miltary Museum

22. Check out the Ludwig Museum

23. Play and learn at this interactive museum

24. Climb up to Schloss Stolzenfles

25. Relax at the garden of Electrol Palace

26. Take the famous Romantic Rhine tour

27. Walk at Lohrstrasse or the city center

28. Walking night tour at Am plan and Munzplatz

30. Enjoy the delicious Ice-Creams

31. . Take advantage of the Rhineland Palatine pass or Koblenz tourist card

32 Explore Trier; UNESCO world heritage city

33. Meet some Animals

34. Spend a day at Burg Eltz

36. Explore Cochem

37. Ride a pedal boat at Lacher See

38. Shopping in Koblenz

39. Pick up things in Sale

40. Shop at Mulheim Karlich

41. Picking up Souvenirs

42. Stock up your personal care products

43. Browse at the second-hand stores

44. Sneak-Peak at Car and train model shops

46. Scream, Shout and Enjoy at the Koblenz Carnival

47. See Rhine in Flames

48. Take a horse ride during Christmas

49. Read a book at a huge Library

50. Note down some important information

Top Reasons to Book This Trip

WHERE WILL YOU TRAVEL TO NEXT?

Our Story

Notes

DEDICATION

This book is dedicated to my husband Jinish Doshi and our daughter Nishi Doshi. It was my husband's decision to settle in this beautiful city; thus giving me an opportunity to pen down my views. Without the support and encouragement of my husband and our lovely daughter; I would have not been able to complete this book.

Hiral Doshi

ABOUT THE AUTHOR

Hiral Doshi loves to travel. Born and raised up in Mumbai (India); the city for Bollywood stars and glamour; she is fond of taking pictures, exploring different places, writing and shopping.

It is been a long time she is shifted with her small family to this new and beautiful city of Koblenz; in Germany. However, during this time she has explored the city with her family and new local friends. She has not only integrated in the city but learnt the local language as well. From being a newbie in a city when she arrived to now walking like a local she has learned many new things in this entire journey.

Hiral Doshi

HOW TO USE THIS BOOK

This book was written by someone who has lived in an area for over three months. The author has made the best suggestions based on their own experiences in the area. Please check that these places are still available before traveling to the area. The goal of this book is to help travelers either dream or experience different locations by providing opinions from a local.

Hiral Doshi

FROM THE PUBLISHER

Traveling can be one of the most important moments in a person's life. The memories that you have of anticipating going somewhere new or getting to travel are some of the best. As a publisher of the Greater Than a Tourist book series, as well as the popular 50 Things to Know book series, we strive to help you learn about new places, spark your imagination, and inspire you.

Thought this book you will find something for every traveler. Wherever you are and whatever you do I wish you safe fun, and inspiring travel.

Lisa Rusczyk Ed. D.
CZYK Publishing

Hiral Doshi

WELCOME TO > TOURIST

Hiral Doshi

INTRODUCTION

Koblenz or also known as Coblenz lies in the wine growing Rhineland Palatine region. It is located in Southwest Germany. Koblenz is easily accessible by Germany's International airport; Frankfurt am Main. There is a direct train from Frankfurt airport to Koblenz. Overall train connectivity for Koblenz is easy; there are direct trains from Paris, Interlaken in Switzerland, Munich; in Germany and many more major cities.

Hiral Doshi

1. Know the history of Koblenz

Koblenz has its history from the ancient times. In 10 BC Romans founded a military stronghold in Koblenz due to its strategic location. This beautiful city is a confluent point of two major rivers of Germany; Rhine and Moselle. Today, this town is an economic and commercial centre of the Upper Rhine region. With a population of about just 1 lakh (as on June 2017); this place attracts many tourists from all over the world all round the year. The town also has beautiful mountain ranges; Hunsruck, the Eifel and Westerwald are some of them. It is not been very long I am living here but I am surely in love with this beautiful city.

2. Visiting Koblenz; plan when to visit

Ideally you can visit this city any time of the year; it is equally beautiful. The winters are not so severe here as in the other cities of Germany. Being near the river; summer days are also cool and pleasant with temperature ranging from about 15 at night to about 23 in the day time. However, there might be couple of very hot days and couple of very cold days; however, they do not last long. It has been in very rare case that Koblenz experience severe snowfall or heavy rain showers. However, do not forget to carry your umbrella and rain wear along with your seasonal clothing as it might rain any time here.

3. Learn basic German

The saying, 'When in Rome do like the Romans do' is true in Germany as well. It is best to learn the basic German so that it helps you to find the basic things here and makes it easy for you to move around. Some of the things you can learn is Days of the Week (Sonntag, Montag, Dienstag, Mittwoch, Donnerstag, Frietag, Samstag); starting from Sunday. This would help you to know the timings of the shops and other places. Some of the other things you can learn is Bahnof is station; Bushaltestelle is the Bus Stop; abfahrt is the time for departure and Gleis is platform. However, English speaking people here are welcomed too. If you can talk Arabish or Turkish; then too you would find many locals.

4. Find a stay in Koblenz

The only option I can think of to explore this beautiful city is to buy a house and stay here. Once you step in here you would not feel like going back. However, unfortunately; the reality is different; everyone who comes here cannot stay here. Being one the well known tourist attractions in Germany; the hotel and apartment industry here has many options for the travellers.

Different types of affordable and luxurious stays are available here. You can find accommodations as low as 30 € per night to as high as 100 € per night. You can select from options like DJH hostel, Aparthotel at Munzplatz, Mercure hotel which is near the Hauptbahnof (main station) and few others. You can select to stay in the Mitte (main city center) or a little far off; this can be locations like Sud-Koblenz, Koblenz Lutzel, Ehrenbreitstein, Metternich area and Mulheim Karlich. From these locations you can easily reach the main station or main market city by bus. Staying in Ehrenbreitstein region has its own charm as it is uphill and hence the temperature is slightly low as compared to the city; the mountains give you a company every morning for your tea and breakfast.

5. Sleep in a caravan or a tent

Along with fancy and luxurious hotels stays and apartments; Koblenz also has an option to sleep in a caravan. It is one of the best options for people who are camping. Yes, you can bring your caravan here or can rent a tent in one of them.

There is a huge camping place in Koblenz-Lutzel. This place is connected with the boat ferry and has good connectivity to the city center as well. The price for renting this place starts from 17 € per night if you have your caravan and if you want to rent a place in a caravan the prices start from 20 € per night. The camping area has a good facility of toilets and bathrooms for your daily shower. There is also a small restaurant which can serve you basic starters and some drinks. A supermarket called Netto is just 5 mins walk from the camping place. It is just at the corner where you need to bend to reach camping place.You can check the availability and the final prices at Knaus campingpark or Camping park Rhein Mosel.

6. Eat and shop groceries like a local

There are many grocery stores and supermarkets situated in the city. Some of the known ones are Globus, Lidl, Aldi, Netto, Penny or Rewe. Most of them have a good connectivity with a local bus. Lidl and Netto are reasonably priced supermarkets. Rewe and Penny are of the same company; however Rewe has more varieties of products but it is on a expensive side.

You can also find good options for Vegans in these supermarkets. Each of these supermarkets has a huge section dedicated to Vegans where you can shop soya products and other such items. There are Bio Supermarkets too available in the area; Alanatura being one of them.

I personally prefer Lidl; due to its competitive price and high quality of fruits and vegetables. Lidl is an award winner for fresh fruits and vegetables. Additionally; there are many Asian and Turkish shops as well to suit your Asian and Turkish taste buds.. You will also find some shops around the city dedicated only to fruits and vegetables. As per my experience; the price of fruits and vegetables is little on a higher side in these shops compared to the supermarket.

7. Eat the German Breakfast

When you are in Germany; you should have a typical German breakfast. Bread is the staple food for Germans and hence you will find Bakeries (also known as Backerei in German) all around the city.

The two popular brands of bakeries include Hoefer, and Schafer; though you will find many small as well. I personally prefer Hoefer. The chocolate lovers can try the well known Nuss-Nougat Croissant or Choco Roll in breakfast. Ham or salami, and different types of cheese with a strong coffee or tea are some of the things included in a typical German breakfast.

In the season of strawberries and cherries you will get an option to choose from strawberry pie or cherry pie. These bakeries bake fresh bread and small cakes every morning and hence do not be shocked to see a line in front of the bakers when you go for a morning walk. Breads are easily available in supermarkets as well; here also they are baked fresh; however, I and many friends here prefer buying from specific bakeries.

8. Shop from the weekly markets

Along with various supermarkets you will also find weekly markets in Koblenz. Here you can pick your favorite fruit, cheese and meat at a reasonable price and of course they are fresh.

Sometimes you can also get International food items. On a chilly winter morning you can enjoy the hot soup sold at these weekly markets. As of now the weekly markets are on Tuesdays and Thursdays at Schloss strasse and on Saturday at Munzplatz from 8.00 am to 2.00 pm.

9. Washing your laundry

You do not need to carry too heavy luggage for your clothes. My town has laundry facilities as well and they are not high on pockets. There are wash salons situated at convenient locations where you can wash and dry your clothes at a reasonable rate. You will also get soap detergent and liquid detergent at these salons. So all you need to do is put them in your bag; roll to the nearest wash salon and let them get washed. You can have a walk around the city when your clothes are being washed. And if you do not want to walk around; you would also find other tourists there with whom you can have your small talks. Sometimes; local students also use these salons.

10. Visit the famous Deutsche Eck

Deutsche Eck is one of the most beautiful attractions of Koblenz; it is also known as heart of Koblenz. The shape of this place is one of the noticing feature. The Eck is shaped like bow of a ship with Rhine river to the east and Moselle to the north. The tip of the Eck would be the exact location where Leonardo DiCaprio would be kissing Kate Winslet if this were at Titanic.

There is a statue of Kaiser Wilhelm 1 on horseback. Kaiser Wilhelm was the beloved Kaiser of Germany. The statue was destroyed in World War 2; however, it was rebuilt again in 1990. The locals here were happy with the reconstruction of the statue. You can climb the stairs and go the foot of this statue. A roman structure is built there and it is very good location for capturing some photographs.

After visiting the statue; you can simply take a stroll down the river front; it is amazing. As a local; on sunny days I do not miss a chance to visit this place. Even after visiting this place innumerable times it looks more beautiful each time I visit. Bus No 1 goes to Deutsche Eck from the main station and city center.

Hiral Doshi

"Traveling – it leaves you speechless,

then turns you into a storyteller."

– Ibn Battuta

Hiral Doshi

11. Walk or ride a bicycle

There is no better way to explore the city on foot or on a bicycle. There is a 15 km bicycle path just below the Balduin bridge near the camping place; this route will take you to Neuweid; a nearby city. Just walking or cycling on this path is a different experience altogether. The best part is that this path is along the river Mosel. A morning walk here or just your regular exercises at this location will rejuvenate your mind and soul.

12. Explore Koblenz through water

You can not only explore Koblenz by foot but also by boat. The river travel is very relaxing and peaceful. There are various options you can take; you can either take a complete day cruise from Koblenz or you can select to take a one hour round trip. With a one day tour you can visit the nearby villages like St. Goar, Boppard and some cities like Mainz, Colonge and Dusseldorf by boat. Generally with your one day ticket you can get down at multiple cities and catch another cruise. However, ensure you check the time table before you start your journey.

The cruise line generally remains closed in winter months October to April. The first cruise begins on Easter Friday. The popular cruise line includes Koln-Dusseldorfer or also known as KD cruise. The ticket price starts anywhere from € 25 for adult for a whole day and kids below 4 years travel free. These cruises will take you through beautiful vineyards, mountains and castles. One hour cruise trip costs anywhere between 7-10 €

13. Enjoy the Cable Car

Once you have completed the boat ride you also have the chance to view Koblenz from in a cable car. Near the Deutsche Eck there is a ropeway or cable car known as 'Sielbahn' which will take you to top of Koblenz. You can also access this location by bus but it is recommended to take the Sielbahn.

The newly designed Seilbahn takes you over the Rhine river, the Kaiser statue and beautiful jungle. If you are lucky you can click pictures of all the modes of transport; train, boat, ropeway, car in one frame. Some of the cable cars have glass bottom so do not forget to sit in one of those.

In winter months these are functional only on weekends and during summers you can visit everyday. Evening tickets are cheaper compared to the day tickets. You can enjoy the cable car with as low as € 7 per person to and fro.

14. View from top

Once you reach at the top with the Sielbahn or bus; there are two main attractions here. First is the Fort Ehrenbreitstein and second is the viewing platform. You need to climb up the platform; it is as high as three storey. This triangular shaped platform gives you a spectacular view of the beautiful town. If you stand at the tip of the platform on the highest floor; you would feel you are just above the valley; there is no support below you. A breeze of fresh air will splash on your face and you can enjoy the best of time. This place also has a huge lawn to sit and relax. Kids can play around. You can take your food and picnic basket to spend your day. The platform is wheel chair and buggy accessible. From here you can take a visit to Fort Ehrenbreitstein.

15. Visit to Fort Ehrenbreitstein

Another attraction of Koblenz is the Fort Ehrenbreitstein; UNESCO; world heritage site since 2002. This marvellous fort is built on a hill named; Ehrenbreitstein. The magnificent fort has a history dating back to 3rd century BC when Romans ruled the place. Earlier as a castle, hiding place for weapons, refugee center, hostel and now to historical museums; this fort has long history. You can view museums like Haus der Fotografie (photography), and Haus der Archäologie (archaeology).

Also known as 'Festung Koblenz' it is the place where many events takes place during summer months. The fort is operational from 10.00 to 18.00 hrs in the months of April to October and from 10.00 to 17.00 hrs in the months of November to March. You would require one complete day to witness the fort. The entry ticket is € 7; however, you can combine with the combi-ticket of Sielbahn and can enjoy both at a good price.

16. Drink at Bier Garten at Deutsche Eck

After you come down from visiting the marvelous Fort you can relax yourself at this location. The name itself is enough to know what this place is about. If you are thinking; why am I mentioning it here as you can easily find this when you are at Deutsche Eck? The reason I am listing here is because this is one of the best place where you can sit and enjoy your beer at a reasonable price and in peace. You are in middle of river Rhine and Mosel. While sipping the beer in summers a cool wave of wind blows on your face. If you have a lucky day; you could see some huge swans enjoying in the water.

17. Splash in the Heat

If you visit Koblenz in summer time; one of the best seasons then your kids can enjoy the water play area near Deutsche Eck. This play area is designed in such a way to not only enjoy and play with water but kids also learn some basic things how would a dam work and similar. You can get an extra pair of clothes for your kids as once they go in they are surely would be wet and you would have to drag them out. It is fun; I wish I was a kid to enjoy this fun. This place is open till 6.00 pm so you spend your afternoon here. This place is also adjacent to Bier Garten and hence parents can sip beer and kids can enjoy.

18. Visit Schloss Sayan

Schloss Sayan is located in a nearby village of Bendorf. This palace was destroyed in World War 2 and the reconstruction was completed in 2000. Together with the castle hill and the park the neo-gothic residence of the Princes of Sayn-Wittgenstein-Sayn is the centerpiece of a romantic ideal landscape. This Schloss also has a beautiful park with a small lake and kids play area. You can also visit a butterfly park here. The entry to the park is free; however, to visit the butterfly garden you need to pay a fee of 7.50€ for adults and 5 € for kids. The entry to the palace costs 5€ for adults and 3.50 € for kids. A combi ticket is generally cheaper. The palace museum and buttefly park remains open till 6.00 pm in summer months and in winters upto 5.00 pm. Bus no 8 from Forum Zentralplatz will take you to Schloss (last stop).

19. Walk on the longest Suspension Bridge

Since October 2015; Germany has its longest suspension bridge at Geierlay. The bridge is located near the small town of Mörsdorf about 50 kms from Koblenz. The suspension bridge is 360 m long and 100m high. You can reach here by car or by combination of bus and train with a change possible at Kastellaun. Bus no 610 goes to Kastellaun from Koblenz main station and from there catch bus no 634. If you happen to travel in Spring season you can witness the amazing yellow blooming flowers. The entry to the bridge is free; from the Besuch Centrum (Visiting Center), your walk for 1.9 km towards the bridge starts.

The suspension bridge gives you an adrenaline rush. For the first time I was scared but as I started walking I enjoyed. You can also take kids buggy on this bridge; however bulky strollers are not possible. Kids also enjoy the walk; my 2 year old surely did. Take your picnic bag and you can have your lunch on other side of the bridge.

20. Check out some old train models at Deutsche Bahn Musuem

The city not only has wonderful river front but it also has a train museum also known as Deutsche Bahn museum. As the name suggests here you can see variety of trains right from olden times. The train models are displayed in such a way that you can take a look from the interiors as well. On some of the days there are parades held where you would see the original train engines moving; literally a train parade.

You would also get a chance to see the miniature trains inside the museum and yes it is fun place for kids as well. The entry to this museum is not heavy on the pocket; for adults it costs 3€ and for kids it is 1,50 €.

Hiral Doshi

"Travel is more than the seeing of sights;
it is a change that goes on, deep and
permanent, in the ideas of living."

– Miriam Beard

Hiral Doshi

21. Sneak Peak at Miltary Museum

Miltary museum or also known as Wehrtechnische Studiensammlung; Koblenz. This amazing museum is a must visit in Koblenz. This 4 storey museum has a huge collection of military tanks, guns, communication systems, air planes and other things. All of this year is in perfect working condition. You can enter this museum at a unbelievable price of 3€. I have never visited a museum with so low entrance ticket. Do not forget to carry your passport while you make a visit here. You can take bus no 5 from Koblenz main station or any buses going to Lutzel station will get you at this museum.

22. Check out the Ludwig Museum

The Ludwig Museum of Koblenz is one of five museums in Germany, which was founded by the famous collector couple Peter and Irene Ludwig. Since its opening in december 1992, the museum defines itself by an active dialogue in modern art with France. This museum is open from Tuesdays to Saturdays from 10.30 am to 5.00 pm and on Sundays and holidays from 11.00 am to 6.00 pm. The entry to this museum is 5 € for adults.

23. Play and learn at this interactive museum

Do not miss to visit the Romanticum museum here. Unlike the traditional museum; this one is an interactive exhibition. At this center you can bring life to every fascinating aspect of the romantic Middle Rhine Valley over an area of 800 m². You can enjoy the fantastic journey through time as a steamship passenger and experience the pure romance of the Rhine up along with knowing the history of river Rhine. The gallery is open daily from 10.00 am to 6.00 pm. You can enter this museum with a nominal price of 6 €.

24. Climb up to Schloss Stolzenfles

Stolzenfels is another castle built on the banks of the river in Koblenz. The castle is accessible by bus no. 650 going towards Boppard. This castle is located on hilltop and hence you would have to walk out your way for about 2-3 kms. The route is worth walking up. Once you are on top; the view is mesmerizing where you see beautiful forest down and a flowing river. The castle is operational from mid March to end of October from 10.00 AM to 5.00 PM and in winter months it is operational only on weekends. The entry to the castle is 5 € for adults and you can enter this castle only with a guided tour.

25. Relax at the garden of Electrol Palace

The Electrol Palace was one of the last residential palaces that was built in Germany just before the French revolution. It is one of the most important buildings in Koblenz. The unique French Classical style is relevant in the construction of this palace. Today, the palace has exclusive banquet halls for wedding and other parties. You can enjoy your tea at the Grand Café and what more you can enter free at the beautiful garden terrace which is located near the river side.

26. Take the famous Romantic Rhine tour

River Rhine cuts deeply through mountains, valleys, hillside and castles in the area between Rudesheim and Koblenz. One can also witness the steep fields of wine producing areas. The entire Rhine tour area is listed in UNESCO as a world heritage site since 2002. Once on Rhine tour you can witness half-timbered houses, Gothic churches and castles right from the fairy tale world. These medieval castles were built by knights, robber barons, princes and bishops. Today, some of these castles are open for public while some are now turned into hotels for tourists. You can buy a day pass at the counter at Deutsche Eck and enjoy the romantic Rhine valley tour.

27. Walk at Lohrstrasse or the city center

This place is not only the shopping hub of Koblenz; but also one of the main junctions from where you can get buses for most of the direction. There is also a small station named as Koblenz; Stadt- Mitte. The name itself says; Koblenz (main center). There is a huge shopping mal here; named as Lohr Center. Just outside this mall there is a bus depot where multiple buses stop. Walking ahead of this road; you can see Vier Turme (four towers) at the intersection of Altengraben. These towers are 17-century buildings with detailed carvings. They are definitely picture taking spots. Once you cross the road you can also see some small beautiful fountains.

28. Walking night tour at Am plan and Munzplatz

This is square in the city center. This huge square is well known for its restaurants and ice-cafes. If you visit this place in summers you would see people sitting in outdoor restaurants and enjoying the sun. Just a walking tour at night at this location is amazing. The area is light up with different lights and the atmosphere is completely different. On the days of events in the city; this is the main area for attraction.

Munzplatz is another area where you can sit and enjoy; you need not be in any restaurant. A public square constructed with beautiful fountain in the middle makes this place attractive for many locals as well. The kids have ample place to play and the parents take spend quality time with each other. These places are car free zones.

29. Eating in Koblenz

Cooking on your own is the best option to save on cost; however, there is no harm in trying out the local food. Here in Koblenz; you would not only get German restaurants but you would find many restaurants with International cuisine. You name it and we have it. You can enjoy the meal at the river front restaurants and within the city as well. Doner Kebabs, varieties of Cheese and Plfammkuchen are some of the things to try out here.

30. Enjoy the delicious Ice-Creams

If you are visiting this beautiful city in summer months or on a sunny day you would definitely find people walking besides you are having scoops of ice creams. Yes, I literally mean 'Scoops.' Its been long and I have not seen people here eating just one scoop of ice cream. I do not blame them but the ice creams here are just amazing. You just cannot have just ONE scoop. There are many ice cream parlors here and you would find varieties of fresh ice creams.

You can also have a complete Ice-cream Becher (like a sundae). I would recommend you to taste the Spaghetti Ice cream in Koblenz. It is my favorite; especially in the strawberry season. You can definitely find me at one of the ice-cream café on weekends if the sun is shining.

Hiral Doshi

There are no foreign lands. It is the traveler only who is foreign."

– Robert Louis Stevenson

Hiral Doshi

31. . Take advantage of the Rhineland Palatine pass or Koblenz tourist card

In order to explore Koblenz at a discounted rate; you can take a Koblenz Tourist card. On this card you not only get free access to local transportation but also huge discounts at various museums, cable car rides, boat trips and similar other. You can also enjoy a free guide tour through Koblenz. The card costs 9.80 €; however, you can keep checking the Koblenz tourism website there are attractive deals as well for the card.

You can also explore the entire Rhineland- Palatine region by purchasing Rhineland Palatine pass. This pass is valid for one day and you can travel within the state in any regional transportation at free of cost.

32 Explore Trier; UNESCO world heritage city

Trier is yet another city in Rhineland Palatine region; it lies at the bank of the River Moselle. The city is close to Luxembourg. This city is not only known for its wine producing areas but also for its Roman architecture. Porta Nigra, Imperial Roman Baths, Ampitheatre are some of the major attractions. Once you reach Trier station; you can catch bus and reach various locations. Most of the buses will go to Porta Nigra. From there you can follow the Tourist path; relevant markings are there. I would suggest to take a bus to Ampitheatre as it is little bit far and uphill. A visit to Trier is cost effective when you purchase the Rhineland Palatine pass with this pass you can enjoy free transportation in the buses in Trier as well.

33. Meet some Animals

Animal lovers can meet some animals at the famous Neuweid Zoo. This Zoo not very far from Koblenz and has a wide species of animals and birds. Leopards, Chimpanzees, monkeys, Penguins are some of the animals you can see here. The Zoo also has a very nice Kinderland or Kids play area. With an entry of 12 € you can enjoy at this zoo; a perfect place for a family picnic. The Zoo is open from 9.00 AM to 6.00 PM in summers and from 9.00 AM to 5.00 PM in winters. However, the entry closes one hour before the closing time. A combination of bus and train will take you to this Zoo.

34. Spend a day at Burg Eltz

A visit to the famous Burg Eltz is no less than a fairy tale. If you happen to visit this castle during the blooming season the view is just mesmerizing. The castle is unique; it was safe in the war. The architecture of this castle is unique and till date you can find many of the orginal carvings from eight centuries in place. The Eltz family still lives in there. The castle is built on a high on a large rock, but in a valley. It is surrounded by the Eltz Forest. You can definitely hike area as the hiking area is the award-winning dream hike "Eltz Castle Panorama."

To reach the castle you can take a bus from Münstermaifeld and Wierschem and on weekends and public holidays you can take the ÖPNB "Burgenbus" or you can simply drive. The castle is open daily from 9.30 am to 5.30 pm. The informative guided tour of the castle costs 10 €. You cannot enter the castle without a guided tour. For foreign speakers there are translations available and tours in English, French and Dutch can be organized as per request. However, as my experience if you go on weekends they generally have a English guided tour every half an hour.

35. Visit UNESCO heritage site; Marksburg castle

Marksburg castle is a UNESCO world heritage site of the upper middle Rhine Valley. The castle along the Rhine river was never destroyed in war. It can also be termed as virtually unchanged from Medieval times. The entry to the castle is only possible with a 50 minute guided tour. English guided tours are conducted everyday at 1.00 PM and at 4.00 PM in the summer season. The castle is open from 11.00 AM to 5.00 PM in summers and from 10.00 AM to 4.00 PM in winters. The entry is 7 € and you can avail the group discounts. This castle is not accessible by buggys or wheelchairs hence; people with kids can park their buggy outside and carry a baby carrier with them for easy movement. You can either catch a train or bus to Braubach; it will take 10-20 minutes.

36. Explore Cochem

Cochem is another beautiful medieval town in Rhineland Palatine region. The Cochem castle, Old town are some of the things not to be missed in Cochem. The town can be seen on foot; however, you can also take a small city train at 7 € per person. This mini-train also has guided audio tours in various languages. Another attraction in Cochem is the "Sesselbahn" or also known as Chair Lift car. This open chair lift takes you up the hill from where you can enjoy the beautiful view of the city. A return journey costs about 5 € per person. The experience of witnessing the forest and river below your feet is very nice. My 2 year old kid enjoyed herself.

37. Ride a pedal boat at Lacher See

This is an unexplored site near Koblenz. As a tourist; many would miss it but as a local I suggest to visit this place. A beautiful volcanic lake with diameter of 2 km gives you a serene feeling. A pedal boat ride in this lake is a must for your relaxation. You can reach this lake from Andernach station. You can catch a train from Koblenz to Andernach and a bus would take you to Lacher See. There is also a small wandering path midst the forest.

38. Shopping in Koblenz

Inspite of being a small city; it has many brands and sufficient shops. The town has shops for low-budget college students and for high class professionals as well. If you are low on budget and are looking for something economical with a decent quality; you can go in to C&A. It is right opposite to Forum Zentral. Other high end shops include H&M, Zara, S.Oliver, White Stuff and many more. There are two main malls in Koblenz; Lohr Center and Forum Confluentes. The "Forum Confluentes" is designed by German-Dutch star architects Benthem-Crouwel, is considered to be an architectural masterpiece.

39. Pick up things in Sale

When you see the board of sale or "Rabatt", or "Alles Muss Raus" at the entrance of any shop; then take a visit to the store. The sale in Koblenz has the real meaning and there have been times where I have shopped my winter jackets at as low as 10 € and a knee length dress at 5€. Generally, these 'Sale' boards are red in color in Koblenz and here when I see red I do not stop; but enter inside.

40. Shop at Mulheim Karlich

For shopping freaks like me; you should make a visit to a area called Mulheim Karlich in Koblenz. Bus no 370 will take you to Mulheim Karlich area. Here you will find various brands of shoes, bags, clothes, furniture and many other products. Sometimes, you really get very nice deal in this location. The best deal I have got till date is very good quality 3 T-shirts and 2 Shorts in 8€. I would suggest to carry a Google map with you during your visit. This area is very big and has hundreds of shops; so Google maps could help you to find your desired shop.

Hiral Doshi

"It is good to have an end to journey toward; but it is the journey that matters, in the end."
— *Ursula K. Le Guin,*

Hiral Doshi

41. Picking up Souvenirs

Along with memories from Koblenz; you can take home some Koblenz Souvenirs. The best ones would be with the Deutsche Eck on the same. Magnets, cups and many more options are available. You can easily get them at the stores in the city center. Apart from souvenirs; you can also pick up some wine as the area is known for wine industry. There are shops in Lohr center and Forum mall from where you can pick up your wine stocks.

42. Stock up your personal care products

Germany is well known for its personal care products for both men and women. In Koblenz there branded shops like Body Shop, Yves Rocher and drogerie markets like Muller, and Rossmann which would fetch you very good deals in Perfumes and personal care products. Germany as a country has very high standard of beauty products available across Europe and hence taking them along with you is a great gift for your loved ones as well. You can select from a wide range of beauty products; including handmade products available in the Forum Mall. My guests always have one list ready for their shopping.

43. Browse at the second-hand stores

There are various second hand stores in Koblenz as well.
Some of them include Oxfam; where your spending goes for a
donation. Second-style shop located at Löhrrondell street is for
high end brands, Max & Moritz is specially for kids products and
there are few more around the street. At these second hand shops
you can get very good quality antique furniture, clothes, toys and
many more things. I take a look at them atleast once in a fortnight.

44. Sneak-Peak at Car and train model shops

Germany is the favorite destination for car lovers. Along with the world famous Autobahn; the cars of Germany are also well known amongst the enthusiasts. Koblenz is place for antique car and train lovers. We have a huge shop at Löhrondel strasse for Car models and train models. There are two different shops for each one of them; however, both are located next to each other. You can find very old cars and trains here. You can also find some good deals in second hand model cars and model trains.

45. Shop at the Holland market

If you happen to visit Koblenz in the month of March then you can take advantage of the Holland market. The locals here wait very eagerly for the entire here for this market. In this market you can find that wholesalers and manufactures from Holland bring high quality cloth for stitching. Along with a wide variety of cloth rolls you would also fine innumerable variety of clothing accessories; buttons, bows, fancy ribbons and the list is endless. Needless to say things are very reasonably priced here and are of high quality.

46. Scream, Shout and Enjoy at the Koblenz Carnival

The carnival time in Koblenz is the Shrove Monday. The event starts at the eleventh hour of the eleventh day of the eleventh month. Ideally as per regular calendar this event falls in end of February to mid March. There are numerous street shows, performances organized in this week. The celebration starts from Thursday- Weiberfastnacht (women's carnival) upto Ash Wednesday. You would see most of the disco's and pubs have events in these days. On Shrove Monday there is a huge parade in the city center of Koblenz. The kids do enjoy and so do we. The beautifully made air balloons and amazingly dressed people are the highlight of the parade. The Germans are said to be the quiet people but on this day; they scream, shout and enjoy. They scream by saying, "Oolaao." The visitors are also dressed up in a unique way.

47. See Rhine in Flames

This is a yearly festival in Koblenz. It takes place in second weekend of August. The festival lasts for three days and is the biggest festival of the year in Koblenz. One first two days you would see various bands are performing along the Rhine river and there will be a major band at the Deutsche Eck. You can also find some activities for the kids; carousel, merry go round and few other small games.

On the last day of this festival; there is a huge fireworks show up in the Fort Ehrenbreitstein. Of course you can witness this fireworks show from Deutsche Eck or from the camping area. As per the name on this day; the river Rhine is in Flames and completely lit up. People from nearby cities take a visit on this day for this event. You can also enjoy a dinner boat ride and witness the entire event from the boat. This is definitely a grand event.

48. Take a horse ride during Christmas

A visit to Koblenz in the Christmas month is definitely worth it. The streets are light up from the start of the Advent month till mid of January of the New Year. With more than thousand lights and decoration on the streets; the regular streets are no more the same. There is an aroma of celebration everywhere. The six main locations for the Christmas market are; Münzplatz, Plan, Rathausplatz, Liebfrauenkirche, Jesuitenplatz, Zentralplatz), traditional gingerbread hearts, a blaze of lights and literature classics: one of Germany's oldest cities is turned into a Christmas paradise in the Advent season, ideal for strolls around the city. Do not miss the traditional Gluh Wien in the market. The city attracts more than 3,00,000 visitors from all over the country during this time. I always thought Koblenz was the most beautiful city; but after seeing the city light up in Christmas lights I am sure; beautiful is a very small word to describe this city. It is extra-ordinary.

49. Read a book at a huge Library

This small city has a three storied library or also known as Bibliothek. The library has a huge collection of book for each age group. However, you would find most of the books in German but there is a huge collection of English books and other foreign language including French, Dutch, Arabic and many other. On the ground floor you can find various business and other magazines in different language. On third floor you can find books in English. However, if you have some books you can surely sit there and read; you need not borrow one from there. The relaxing chairs in the library makes your reading a pleasant experience. You can also sip a cup of coffee from the café. In summer months you can take advantage of the open lounge or terrace with a minimal fee of approximately 1 €.

50. Note down some important information

Lastly, I would like to share some important details which might be helpful for your visit to Koblenz. The basic helpline numbers for fire and ambulance is 112; for Police is 110. The country code is +49. There are Apothek's (pharmacist) located across the city for your local medicines. The general doctor would be above these Apothek. However, for emergencies you can visit the Krankenhaus (hospitals) for medical reasons. The Apothek would be closed on Sunday but there would always be a label outside the door for an alternative Apothek on a holiday; you can check out the entrance.

The post offices are open from 8.00 am to 6.00 pm on Monday- Friday and till 1.00 pm on Saturday. Restaurants are generally open till 11.00 PM. The super markets and bakeries start from as early as 7.30 AM and are operational till 9.00 PM in most cases. However, the shops in cities closes down at 6.00 PM only the shops in Forum mall are open till 8.00 PM. All shops and supermarkets are closed on Sundays; only bakeries are open till noon. Restaurants and clubs are operational on Sundays as well. Finally, enjoy your stay at Koblenz; have a safe and a memorable vacation.

Hiral Doshi

Top Reasons to Book This Trip

- Wine producing region: Best wine vineyards
- Food: The food is amazing.
- Historic Importance: A rich heritage of tradition.

Hiral Doshi

> TOURIST

GREATER THAN A TOURIST

Visit GreaterThanATourist.com
http://GreaterThanATourist.com

Sign up for the Greater Than a Tourist
Newsletter
http://eepurl.com/cxspyf

Follow us on Facebook:
https://www.facebook.com/GreaterThanATourist

Follow us on Pinterest:
http://pinterest.com/GreaterThanATourist

Follow us on Instagram:
http://Instagram.com/GreaterThanATourist

Hiral Doshi

> TOURIST

GREATER THAN A TOURIST

Please leave your honest review of this book on Amazon and Goodreads. Thank you.

We appreciate your positive and negative feedback as we try to provide tourist guidance in their next trip from a local.

> TOURIST

GREATER THAN A TOURIST

You can find Greater Than a Tourist books on Amazon.

Hiral Doshi

> TOURIST

GREATER THAN A TOURIST

WHERE WILL YOU TRAVEL TO NEXT?

Hiral Doshi

> TOURIST

GREATER THAN A TOURIST

Our Story

Traveling is a passion of this series creator. She studied abroad in college, and for their honeymoon Lisa and her husband toured Europe. During her travels to Malta, an older man tried to give her some advice based on his own experience living on the island since he was a young boy. She thought he was just trying to sell her something. When traveling to some places she was wary to talk to locals because she was afraid that they weren't being genuine. She created this book series to give you as a tourist an inside view on the place you are exploring and the ability to learn what locals would like to tell tourist. A topic that they are very passionate about.

Hiral Doshi

> TOURIST

GREATER THAN A TOURIST

Notes

Printed in Great Britain
by Amazon